THE PELICANS

The Natural History Press, publisher for The American Museum of Natural History, is a division of Doubleday & Company, Inc. The Press is directed by an editorial board made up of members of the staff of both the Museum and Doubleday. The Natural History Press has its editorial offices at The American Museum of Natural History, Central Park West at Seventy-Ninth Street, New York, New York 10024, and its business offices at 501 Franklin Avenue, Garden City, New York 11530.

By George Laycock

THE PELICANS

George Laycock

Published for
THE AMERICAN MUSEUM OF NATURAL HISTORY
The Natural History Press
Garden City, New York

THE PELICANS

THE PELICAN is a famous bird who lives beside the ocean and goes fishing whenever he is hungry. If you should meet a pelican, you will recognize him at once because nothing else looks like a pelican.

His feet are big and flat, and when he walks across the beach, they flap in the sand. His toes are all connected with a web of tough dark skin. This makes walking difficult. When he walks he waddles. Pelicans almost never run. But his webbed feet are just right when the pelican goes swimming. The webs turn his feet into paddles, and pelicans need paddles to push themselves around when they are swimming.

But it is the pelican's head that has made him most famous. His neck is long and crooked, and the bones in it are shaped so he can't straighten his neck out if he wants to. His beak, or bill, is one of the longest among the birds; it is as long as his head and neck together. The pelican carries it resting flat against his neck. When he is standing up, the bill points down at the ground. And when he flies his head comes back to rest between his shoulders. The long, slender bill points out in front of him like a spear.

Strangest of all about the pelican's head, however, is the pouch he carries folded up beneath his bill. No matter how strange this may look to others, it is just the thing a big bird needs if he gets his food by going fishing. And the pelican is a mighty fisherman. That pouch is his dip net, and the pelican uses it to scoop fish out of the ocean.

The top of the dip net is fastened to the bottom of the pelican's bill, and the back of it is fastened down the sides of the big bird's neck. It reaches halfway down his neck. The pouch is made of pelican skin, and there are no feathers on it. It is blackish, soft, and stretchable. When a pelican catches fish in his pouch, he also catches a lot of water. Then, he floats there on the ocean, lowers his bill to let the water drain out of his mouth, Next he tilts his head up and swallows the fish. This way, he doesn't have to swallow the water too.

The brown pelican is only partly brown. His wings and back are lined with silver. And when he is about three years old he grows a new set of feathers that give him his handsome adult colors. His neck is striped with chocolate brown and pure white. He wears a yellow patch at the base of his throat and a golden crown on his head. His yellow eyes are like shiny gems at the front of his head.

The pelican's feathers are his raincoat. No matter how much he dives, and swims, or even sleeps on the water, his feathers stay dry. He keeps them oiled. At the base

of his tail he carries an oil gland as do most birds. He can reach it with the hooked tip of his long bill, and he grooms his feathers and primps and preens with the aid of that bill.

Inside, the pelican is almost as unusual as he is on the outside. Much of a pelican is nothing but air. His bones are hollow, and very thin and strong. This makes them light in weight, which is a good idea for a heavy bird that must fly a lot. But the pelican is also built for floating. His skin and body are so filled with air cells that he can't sink if he wants to. When he wants to dive beneath the water's surface, he has to get a high flying start.

All things considered, the pelican is everything a pelican should be to live the life he leads. If he looks like a clown among birds, he never lets this worry him.

Most people like pelicans. One fisherman remembers a special pelican he once had for a friend. He saw the pelican one day while fishing for shrimp. When he sorted the catch from his net, he threw the small fish away and kept the fine shrimp to sell. And as he began throwing little fish back into the ocean, a big brown pelican flapped slowly out across the bay. When the pelican saw the fish falling back into the ocean, he dived straight down on them with a big splash. Here was a new and easy way for the pelican to get his lunch. And the fisherman was glad to have him there because pelicans are more fun to watch than television.

When the pelican had all he wanted to eat, or when the fisherman was not sorting fish, the bird sat on the waves half asleep.

The pelican and the captain learned to know each other very well. The pelican came closer and closer to the boat. Then one morning, when the captain was not sorting fish, and the pelican was hungry and impatient, he flew in and landed on the stern of the boat. Adjusting his feathers, he stood dignified and silent as if he were really the captain of the boat. The man tossed him a fish and from that time on the pelican was not afraid to ride the fishing boat.

Every morning as the fishing boat left the village, the old brown pelican would come winging in slowly across the bay like part of the crew coming to work. The captain would always say, "Hi there, Pelican, how are you this mornin'?" Adult pelicans are silent, so the pelican would say nothing. He would only nod his head up and down a few times as if to reply that everything was fine.

The captain and the pelican were friends for a long time. And the pelican grew bolder and bolder. He even walked around the boat looking for fish. But he always kept one eye on the captain, as if no pelican should trust anyone completely.

One day the big pelican was very hungry. He ate all the fish the captain gave him and was still hungry. It was then that he saw the fine shrimp the captain was saving to sell in town. There was a whole tub of shrimp.

When the captain turned around the next time, many of the shrimp were inside the big pelican and the old bird was eating more as fast as he could scoop them into his big bill.

The captain was furious. He grabbed a broom and, yelling as loud as he could, rushed across the deck after the pelican. He brushed the scrambling pelican with the side of the broom and swept him right off the boat into the ocean. Then, he leaned over the side of the boat and tried to swat the bird again, but the pelican was too far away. The big bird sat there on the water a few seconds, blinking at the captain, and the captain was still yelling and waving the broom around. Then the pelican flew off slowly across the bay. "That was the last I ever saw of him," said the captain. "I hurt his feelings. It was the end of a beautiful friendship."

In another village on the coast of Florida people talk about the pelican that knocked a man down. Every morning the man would walk out on his boat dock with a fish to feed a special pelican. When he saw the man, the pelican would come flying in across the harbor.

As the pelican approached, the man would hold the fish high in the air. The pelican soon learned to grab the fish out of the man's hand and keep right on flying past

him. It was a game they played. The man thought the big pelican was his pet. The pelican did not think about it one way or the other. All he wanted was the fish.

Then, one morning the man decided to play a trick on his pet pelican. Just as the pelican flapped in toward him on those long, broad wings, the man jerked the fish back and hid it behind him. The man had a big smile on his face. But pelicans don't smile, especially when they see a fish vanish in front of them.

Besides that, it was now too late for the clumsy pelican to change his course. He had followed the fish and at the last moment he was heading right for the man. It was the only wreck the pelican had had since he first learned how to fly. He crashed right into the man's face and knocked him down on the boat dock. Quickly the pelican scrambled away and flapped off again across the harbor. He never came back for another fish. If he had to make a crash landing to get his lunch, he would look elsewhere for it.

Perhaps pelicans should be smarter than they are. They've been here long enough to learn a lot of things, A million years seems like a long time. That is about how long men have been on earth. But pelicans had already been here a long time when men came along. A million years ago there were pelicans that looked about like today's model. And thirty or forty million years before that

there were old-fashioned pelicans. Scientists know from studying fossils in the rocks that the pelican family has been around all that time.

Today there are six kinds of pelicans around the world. In America there are two species. Both are big birds that

live around the water. The brown pelican lives near salt water. But his cousin, the white pelican, is often found far inland, living around big lakes.

Before the arrival of the first explorers on American shores brown pelicans lived all the way around the east coast of North America, from North Carolina southward around the Gulf of Mexico and down into Mexico and South America. On the west coast they lived from the shores of California southward into Chile.

Pelicans often travel together. They fly in a straight line. When their leader rises higher into the sky, each pelican behind him comes to the exact place where the leader has risen, and rises also. It is as if the whole line of birds followed a path marked through the sky.

Sometimes they fly only a few feet above the water. The wings of each pelican seem to move at the same time, and they keep an even distance between them. Like expert trick pilots, they fly in tight formation, always following their leader back and forth to the waters where they fish or to the beaches where they rest.

When a male and female go to Pelican Island, Florida, or some other island, to build their nest, the island may already be filled with other pelicans. But pelicans sometimes nest so close together they can almost reach out and touch their neighbors. When they loaf on the beach, they crowd together and all stand around facing the same direction.

They build their nests near the top of the trees but not in very tall trees. And sometimes, if the trees are gone, pelicans build their nests on the ground.

When the old pelicans need sticks to build a nest, they sometimes get the sticks by breaking them from dead limbs. Other times they steal sticks from careless pelicans who aren't watching their nests. This may be why one pelican stands beside the new nest, guarding it while the mate goes searching for building materials. If a strange pelican comes around stealing sticks, it gets whacked with a long hard bill. This should teach a pelican a thing or two about stealing sticks.

That's the way life is in a pelican community. Pelicans live close together as if they preferred it that way. But they can't really trust each other. Pelicans are not civilized.

By laying sticks across other sticks, the old birds build up a strong platform. Then they carry grass and weeds and spread them on the platform. In the middle of the nest the female pushes the materials down with her body to make a little hollow bed which the eggs cannot roll out of easily.

When the nest is finished, the female lays the first egg.

It is not a fine egg of beautiful colors. It is three inches long and has a whitish shell. In the following days she lays one or two more beside it. If the eggs are to hatch, the old birds must keep them warm for four weeks, so they take turns sitting on the nest. They work in shifts, and while one is busy at the nest the other old pelican is fishing or resting. When she comes back, all rested and ready to go to work, she bows to her mate and bobs her head up and down a few times, and as he leaves the nest she steps onto it gently and settles her warm body over the eggs.

Pelicans need a lot to eat, and when one leaves the nest about the first thing he does is go fishing. He only knows one way to go fishing.

First, he has to find the fish. He cruises along above the water turning his head this way and that. He is always watching the water for a flash of white that shows him where a fish is. He is not much interested in big fish. Usually he hunts menhadden or some other little fish. The fish pelicans eat are not the kinds people usually want.

The deeper the fish are swimming, the higher the pelican must start his dive. He half folds his wings, tips his body forward, and heads down toward the fish. This works best when the wind is behind him, pushing. The farther he falls, the faster he goes. At the last instant he folds his wings in close and takes a belly smacker that

sounds like a board whacking the water. Water splashes up all around him and sparkles in the sunlight. Sometimes he catches the fish. Other times, like fishermen everywhere, he misses.

If he started high enough, and the wind pushed hard enough, the pelican may have been able to go beneath the water. Most often, however, he smacks against the top of the water and stays there. Next he has to turn around and face into the wind. This way he is ready for a fast take-off. Like an airplane, he has to take off into the wind so the wind helps lift his heavy body. When he is ready to fly he gets a running start by standing up and kicking both feet against the surface of the water at the same time, and flapping his long strong wings.

Most of the time the pelican is not alone when he goes fishing. The pesky little laughing gulls are often there to steal his fish, if they get half a chance. And they can be so quick about it, they may have grabbed the fish and gone before the befuddled old pelican knows what happened to him.

The bold laughing gulls swim around the pelican when he has fish in his pouch. Sometimes a gull even sits on the pelican's head. The pelican doesn't seem to mind having a gull on his head. He just sits here, blinking his big eyes and letting the water drain out of his pouch, waiting until he can swallow the fish without the salt water.

But the gull is alert every second. If the fish slips part way out of the pouch, the gull may grab it and pull it away from the pelican. And sometimes a gull will even reach into the pelican's pouch to grab a squirming fish. The pelican still just sits there, blinking, as if it is perfectly natural for him to give away his dinner.

Every meal is the same for the pelican—fish, fish, fish. Even little pelicans get fish for every meal. Little pelicans are not very pretty by human standards. They are wrinkled and they have no feathers. Their eyes are closed for the first two days, and they are too weak to hold up their heads.

Soon the young pelicans are covered with white fluffy feathers. Within five weeks they are old enough to leave the nest. Meanwhile the old birds have been fishing every day and bringing food to the young pelicans. For each young pelican they raise, the old birds must catch and deliver about 150 pounds of fresh fish for it to eat. Young pelicans are fed on fish the old birds have swallowed, partly digested, and regurgitated. Pelicans do not carry fish in their pouches.

Pelicans are not full grown until they are about three years old. Then they have all their fine colors and are old enough to raise families of their own. They are likely to live for many years. In zoos pelicans have lived as long as thirty years.

The most famous place where pelicans live is Pelican Island, the little island on the east coast of Florida. Pelicans have been crowding onto this island to nest for more than a hundred years. That is why it is called Pelican Island. But it is also famous for another reason.

In 1903, pelicans were having great troubles. As usual, their troubles were caused by people. Ladies in those times liked to wear bird feathers on their hats. The feathers came from birds of many kinds, including pelicans. There had been so many pelicans killed for their feathers that they were almost all gone. But people who liked pelicans had an idea.

They took their plan to the President of the United States, Theodore Roosevelt. The President liked their idea. "We'll leave that little island," he said, "for the pelicans." He signed an order that Pelican Island was to be a bird refuge.

It became the first of many National Wildlife Refuges, and it is still a refuge today for the pelicans and other birds.

People and pelicans lived close together for so long that neither one paid much attention to the other. The people went about their daily work in their villages and on their fishing boats. They saw the pelicans, just as they saw the water and the sunshine. The big clumsy birds were part of the world down beside the ocean's edge.

It looked as if this situation might go on and on. But suddenly about 1960, the pelicans were in serious trouble again. People began noticing that few pelicans came around the boat docks or the villages. In fact, there were no pelicans at all in many places.

People who like pelicans are sad about this. It seems that people worry most about pelicans after the pelicans are gone.

Once there were thousands of pelicans nesting and fishing and loafing along the shores of Texas. Suddenly, about 1960, the pelicans went away from Texas and there were no more there to nest and raise young pelicans.

In Louisiana people are also worried about their pelicans. Years ago, the people of Louisiana decided the pelican should be their state bird. They put a picture of a pelican on their great seal. And they put the picture of a pelican on all the automobile license plates sold in Louisiana. They told everyone that Louisiana was the Pelican State.

Then suddenly the pelicans were all gone from the Pelican State. It is sad to have a state bird that won't live in the state. People began looking for ways to get their pelicans back.

Meanwhile, over in Florida, there seemed to be as many pelicans as ever. But the wildlife workers in Florida became very uneasy. If pelicans could disappear from Texas and Louisiana, perhaps they might vanish from Florida too. So they decided to do what they had never done before—they would try to understand their pelicans better. They would search for ways to help these ancient birds live better in these modern times.

Then they began to realize that they did not know much about the pelicans at all. They did not even know how many pelicans lived in Florida. And unless they could find out how many pelicans they had, they wouldn't even know if the pelicans began to disappear. So the wildlife workers decided to fly around the coast of Florida and count pelicans.

On a bright morning in spring, their little airplane left the airport. Inside the airplane were two men. Both were very busy. The pilot was busy piloting, and the passenger was busy looking through his binoculars. After a while he could see a little island far below. He lowered his binoculars and studied his map. Then, smiling broadly, he shouted something to the pilot above the engine's roar. The pilot looked out his window, then turned to the wildlife worker beside him and nodded happily.

At the same time he pushed the steering wheel forward and banked the little plane to the left. The island, far below them, looked very small. For several minutes the plane made great circles above it. Lower and lower it came toward the island. At last the birds noticed the plane coming closer and they shifted nervously A few of the wilder ones lifted up on heavy wings and flapped off across the bay.

Finally, the little airplane straightened out, flew off across the bay, and circled back. The man with the binoculars wanted a very close look at the island.

On the island the birds saw them coming again. There were egrets, herons, gulls, and cormorants. Some birds lifted from the island like a snowstorm. They swirled around in front of the plane, and turned, and wheeled, and sped away.

But the men were more interested in the big brown

birds—the pelicans. Some of them were flying around the island. Others were sitting on nests. Some seemed to be trying to make up their minds whether to fly away or sit and wait. The man with the binoculars was counting as fast as he could. He was counting pelicans, and pelican nests. These were the birds he had come to find, and Pelican Island was crowded with pelicans.

After a while the plane flew higher into the sky and the birds settled back to their life on the island. Inside the plane, the man with the binoculars made notes in a book. But he was also watching for other pelicans. Being a pelican counter is not an easy job. Pelicans don't care whether they get counted or not.

There are many islands around the Florida coast where pelicans go to nest. The biologist flying in the little airplane found them and marked each location on a map. When he was finished, people knew about how many pelicans there were. There were, they said, perhaps twenty thousand. That seems like a lot of pelicans.

There are other things the wildlife workers want to know about the pelicans. One puzzle is where the pelicans go between the time they leave Pelican Island, and other nesting places, and the time they come back. And the wildlife workers think they have a tricky way of finding this out.

They are busy studying how to paint pelicans, or mark

them with colored ribbons. They do not plan to catch each pelican and paint the whole bird. They don't want red, yellow, and blue pelicans. They only want spots of them red, yellow, and blue. Then, if they see a pelican with a strange colored spot or ribbon, they can learn something about him. They will know where he started out, because young pelicans from each nesting area can be marked with a different color.

But the biologists had one more plan they wanted to try. Over in Louisiana wildlife workers built a big wire pen near the edge of the Gulf of Mexico. Meanwhile, in Florida, the wildlife workers paid a visit to one of the islands where many pelicans nest. They took a lot of boxes and cages, and they arrived just before the pelicans were old enough to begin flying. The young pelicans on the island were fifty days old. They would begin flying in five more days.

The wildlife workers caught fifty of the young pelicans. They took them to the mainland and put them into a big truck. They they began driving toward Louisiana.

When the new pelicans from Florida were in the pen in Louisiana, the wildlife workers began feeding them fish. Every day they fed them all the fish they could eat, and the young pelicans grew bigger and stronger. They began stretching their long wings as far as they could. And they flapped them for exercise.

Then one of them made his first solo flight and he discovered something very interesting; the pen had no top. He flew up and over the pen, and he was free. Others followed. Louisiana had some wild pelicans again, and the biologists hoped these would stay to build their nests and raise young pelicans. It would take time to tell, because pelicans do not begin nesting until their third year. But people in Louisiana, Florida, Alabama, Mississippi, and Texas think pelicans are worth all the trouble.

If we learn enough about pelicans, and learn it soon enough, we may be able to help them go on living where they have lived for millions of years.

Meanwhile the pelicans don't seem to care one way or the other. They have their pelican things to do. They have to go fishing a lot. Then there is resting too, and nesting, sleeping, and oiling their feathers. And when that's done they can go right on standing in a line watching the waves coming in to wash their feet. That's the simple life the pelican has been leading for forty million years.

Photo Credits

The Florida Development Commission 11, 13, 18, 25, 26-27, 38.
Karl H. Maslowski 4, 7, 40.
George Laycock 6, 14, 15, 17, 20, 23, 30-31, 32, 34, 35, 42, 43, 46-47, 48,
    49, 51, 52-53, 54-55, 56-57, 59.

GEORGE LAYCOCK is the author of THE ALIEN ANIMALS, THE DEER HUNTER'S BIBLE, THE SIGN OF THE FLYING GOOSE and WILD REFUGE. His articles have appeared in many national magazines, including *Sports Illustrated, Audubon, Field and Stream,* and *Outdoor Life.* Since his boyhood on an Ohio farm, he has been interested in animals, taking a degree in wildlife managament from The Ohio State University. He has traveled widely and has visited all parts of our country.